TEACH YOURSELF THE BIBLE SERIES

ACTS

Adventures of the Early Ch...

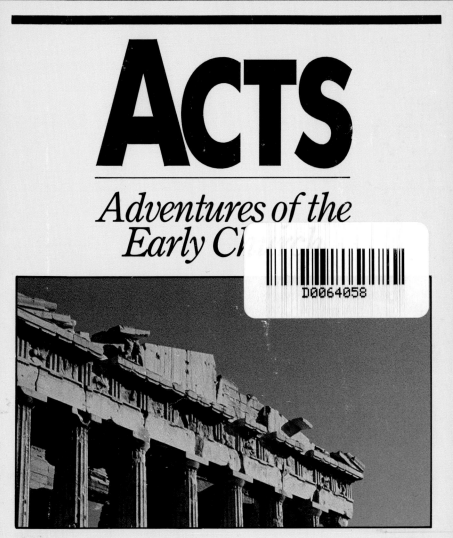

D0064058

The Parthenon on the Acropolis at Athens

KEITH L. BROOKS

The Author used the King James Version when preparing the questions for this manual.

ISBN 0-8024-0125-2

33 34 35 36 Printing/EP/Year 93 92 91 90 89 88

Printed in the United States of America

Acts—Adventures of the Early Church

This is a self-study course designed to help you discover for yourself, from the Bible, some important basic truths concerning the book of Acts.

how to study the lesson

1. Try to find a quiet spot free from distractions and noise.

2. Read each question carefully.

3. Look up the Scripture reference given after each question. Make sure you have found the correct Scripture passage. For example, sometimes you will find yourself looking up JOHN 1:1 instead of I JOHN 1:1.

4. Answer the question from the appropriate Bible passage. Write, in your own words, a phrase or sentence to answer the question. In questions that can be answered with a "yes" or "no" always give the reason for your answer . . . "Yes, because. . . ."

5. If possible, keep a dictionary handy in order to look up words you don't understand.

6. Pray for God's help. You *need* God's help in order to understand what you study in the Bible. PSALM 119:18 would be an appropriate verse for you to take to God in prayer.

7. *Class teachers using this course for group study will find some helpful suggestions on page 95.*

how to
take the self-check tests

Each lesson is concluded with a test designed to help you evaluate what you have learned.

1. Review the lesson carefully in the light of the self-check test questions.

2. If there are any questions in the self-check test you cannot answer, perhaps you have written into your lesson the wrong answer from your Bible. Go over your work carefully to make sure you have filled in the blanks correctly.

3. When you think you are ready to take the self-check test, do so without looking up the answers.

4. Check your answers to the self-check test carefully with the answer key given on page 96.

5. If you have any questions wrong, your answer key will tell you where to find the correct answer in your lesson. Go back and locate the right answers. Learn by your mistakes!

apply
what you have learned
to your own life

In this connection, read carefully JAMES 1:22-25. It is only as you apply your lessons to your own life that you will really grow in grace and increase in the knowledge of God.

Introduction to the Book of Acts

The Writer

This book comes from the same pen as the Gospel of Luke (ACTS 1:1; cf. LUKE 1:3). Examination of the two abundantly confirms this. Traditions of the early church ascribe the book of Acts to Luke.

Acts in several instances refers to incidents mentioned elsewhere in Luke. For instance, the command to tarry in Jerusalem (LUKE 24:49), the return of the eleven to the city after the ascension (LUKE 24:52), the catalogue of the apostles (LUKE 6:14-16), Stephen's prayer (ACTS 7:60) which is an echo of the words of Jesus preserved only by Luke (LUKE 23:34). More than fifty words used in Luke and Acts are not found elsewhere in the New Testament.

The Man

Luke was a physician (COLOSSIANS 4:14). He was Paul's medical adviser and doubtless rescued his life on several occasions. He was a real medical missionary.

Luke was Paul's almost constant companion (PHILEMON 24; II TIMOTHY 4:11). He was with Paul during his second Roman imprisonment, and his devotion to the apostle in the time of peril was beautiful.

The use of medical terms in the description of maladies is a mark both of Luke's Gospel and the book of Acts. In LUKE 4:38 he refers to the high temperature of Simon's wife's mother; in LUKE 8:43, 44 he tells of the hemorrhages of a certain woman; in ACTS 3:7 he explains that the cripple who was lame first received his strength in his feet and ankle bones; in ACTS 12:23 he explains that Herod had worms; in ACTS 13:11 he says that Elymas lost his sight gradually; in ACTS 28:8, speaking of the father of Publius, he mentions his high temperature and bloody issue.

Purpose of the Book

Acts is a continuation of the former treatise. The Gospel of Luke shows the Son of Man at work. Acts shows the Holy Spirit at work. The opening sentences of Acts are an explanation of the closing sentences of Luke. His Gospel records the revelation of the heavenly kingdom and of its foundations in the person and work of the Lord Jesus. Acts describes the royal administration of that kingdom by the power of the Holy Spirit.

In the Old Testament God was at work for man; in the Gospels Christ was at work with man; in the Acts the Holy Spirit was at work in man.

It is a striking fact that Acts records a period of thirty-three years, which was approximately the length of the life of Jesus recorded in the Gospels.

Title of the Book

Our Bible gives the title as "The Acts of the Apostles." It is certain that the author did not give this title. It is not a record of the acts of the apostles, as it contains no detailed account of the work of any apostle except Peter and Paul. It is a record of the workings of the Holy Spirit, who is mentioned about seventy times. "The Acts of the Holy Spirit" would be a good title for this book, for from first to last it is a record of His advent and activity. Men are seen here only as His instruments. In every chapter the careful student will see the Holy Spirit in some aspect of His work. For this reason the book has been called an excellent handbook for soul winners.

Theme of the Book

The theme of this book is clearly stated in ACTS 1:8: "But ye shall receive power, after that the Holy Ghost is come upon you: and ye shall be witnesses unto me both in Jerusalem, and in all Judea, and in Samaria, and unto the uttermost part of the earth." Note particularly that the same gospel which was declared to the Jews was to go to the whole world (cf. MATTHEW 28:19, 20). The book of Acts shows how the teaching of the apostles was begun in each of the appointed fields referred to in verse 8.

Outline of the Book

The Church in Preparation

ACTS 1, 2

The Words of Preparation—Acts 1

"*Ye shall be witnesses*"

Our Lord has two bodies—His literal body and His spiritual body the Church. In his Gospel Luke gives the history of Christ's physical presence among men. In Acts we have the beginning and early history of His spiritual body. Both have a supernatural beginning, a period of service on earth, a final translation into heaven.

1. What is "the former treatise" referred to by Luke?

LUKE 1:1-4 _____

2. What did the "former treatise" record?

ACTS 1:1 _____

The word *infallible* is literally "irresistible." The proofs of the resurrection are indeed irresistible. Delusions do not live long and have no power to lift men Godward. After two thousand years the resurrection is the greatest moral dynamic known.

3. What did Jesus tell His disciples during the forty days before the ascension?

1:3 _____

4. What baptism did Jesus promise?

1:5 _____

If the word *baptism* means a complete submersion, as most authorities agree, the baptism of the Spirit must have reference to the day of Pentecost when the very house in which the disciples were meeting was filled and where tongues of fire sat upon them. Believers were baptized into one body by the Spirit at Pentecost, and all who have since received Christ have participated in that baptism without the necessity of the signs—rushing mighty wind, tongues of fire and speaking in languages unknown to them.

5. For what distinct purpose is the power of the Spirit given to believers?

1:8 _____

6. What is the one method by which Christianity can advance in the world?

1:8 _____

7. What "table of contents" for the book of Acts do you find in

1:8? _____

The important teaching of this verse is that one who participates in the power that originated at Pentecost will reveal it by his great passion to carry the message of salvation to men.

8. What did the disciples do in the upper room?

1:14 _____

9. What woman is specially mentioned as being present?

1:14 _____

This is the last reference to the mother of Jesus. We leave her on her knees in prayer—not being prayed to. With all the others she was baptized into the Church at Pentecost.

10. What prophecy fitted Judas' case exactly?

1:20 _____

_____

11. What must the successor to Judas have witnessed?

1:22 _____

12. What method did the disciples choose to select a successor to Judas?

1:26 _____

13. What preceded the choosing of the successor?

1:24 _____

The Spirit of Power—Acts 2

"They were all filled"

14. What great feast was now due?

2:1 _____

The word *Pentecost* means "fiftieth" (LEVITICUS 23:15, 16). It was observed on the fiftieth day, or seven weeks, from the Paschal feast. It was also called Feast of Weeks (II CHRONICLES 8:12, 13). It marked the completion of the barley harvest, which began at the time of the waving of the first ripe sheaf of first fruits. The Feast of Weeks, therefore, fell on the fiftieth day after this occurrence.

15. What advance sign came from heaven signifying the approach of the Holy Spirit?

2:2 _____

16. What appeal was made to the eye?

2:3 _____

17. Was it really wind, or a "sound as of wind"?

2:2 _____

8

The rushing wind is a portent of the speed of the gospel; the tongues of fire suggest the burning energy which causes believers to proclaim God's wonderful plan of redemption. Tongues of fire suggest man's voice speaking in God's power. Fire throughout the Word is symbolical of the presence of God.

18. Was the baptism of the Spirit for individuals or a body of believers?

I CORINTHIANS 12:13 _____

19. When these believers were "filled," what did they do?

ACTS 2:4, 6, 11 _____

20. Of what benefit was this speaking in tongues?

2:11 _____

Note that "Pentecostal tongues" was a miraculous endowment to enable the first Christians to declare the glad tidings to those whom they could not otherwise reach. Thus the precious seed was given out, carried to sections from whence these people had come, and a great harvest sprang up in many places.

21. Another such manifestation was given later to what group?

ACTS 10:44-46 (see verse 24) _____

22. What signs were repeated on that occasion?

_____

The event of Pentecost remains. The indwelling Spirit is with all believers now as much as with the early Christians, and will as readily fill us and use us if we will yield to Him. The essential fact is that believers are filled that they might witness to others.

23. How do you account for the great change in Peter?

ACTS 2:14; compare JOHN 18:27 _____

24. From whose prophecy did Peter quote?

ACTS 2:16 _____

25. Does this prophecy have further fulfillment?

JOEL 2:30, 31 _____

Some teach that the phenomenon of Pentecost was identified with Joel's prophecy (JOEL 2:28, 29) as the same in kind, but not the same in degree, since the prophecy declares that the Spirit should be poured out upon all flesh. Thus, it is said, Pentecost was an anticipation of what will take place at the second coming of Christ.

On the other hand, we know of no Scripture which teaches that every individual in the Kingdom Age will prophesy, etc., even to daughters and old men. The present age would seem to be the logical time for prophesying (lit. "forth-telling"). The words *all flesh* suggest to some students the thought that all classes, without distinction of age, sex, nation, or standing, will be used by the Holy Spirit.

26. What great truths did Peter expound in this sermon?

ACTS 2:22, 23 _____

2:24 _____

2:31 _____

2:36 _____

27. Why was Jesus raised from the dead?

2:24 _____

28. What did David foresee would happen to the Messiah before He should sit on a throne?

2:27, 30 _____

29. What happened when the people heard Peter's sermon?

2:37 _____

10

30. What must a person do to be saved?

2:38 _____

31. To whom is the promise of the Holy Ghost given?

2:39 _____

32. What did the believers do in order to grow in their Christian lives?

2:42 _____

33. What ordinance was practiced by the early church?

2:42 _____

34. What was the general atmosphere of the church?

2:46 _____

35. Who makes the real additions to the church?

2:47 _____

check-up time No. 1

You have just studied some important truths about Acts 1, 2. Review your study by rereading the questions and your written answers. If you aren't sure of an answer, reread the Scripture portion given to see if you can find the answer. Then take this test to see how well you understand important truths you have studied.

In the right-hand margin write "True" or "False" after each of the following statements.

1. The book of Acts was written by the apostle Paul. _____

2. Jesus commanded the disciples to leave Jerusalem after the ascension.   _____

3. Jesus promised them the baptism of the Holy Ghost. _____

4. The disciples were to witness first in Jerusalem.   _____

5. Matthias was appointed to take the place of Judas. _____

6. The Holy Spirit came on the Day of Atonement.   _____

7. Men from many countries heard the gospel proclaimed in their own language.   _____

8. Peter said that the prophecy of Isaiah was being fulfilled.   _____

9. David prophesied concerning the resurrection of Jesus Christ.   _____

10. Very few were converted by Peter's first sermon. _____

Turn to page 96 and check your answers.

The Church in Action

ACTS 3–5

The Apostles' Preaching—Acts 3
"Repent ye"

1. After Pentecost Peter and John joined with the Jewish church in what hour?

3:1 _____

2. What did the lame man receive instead of alms?

3:7 _____

3. What possession is worth more than money?

3:6 _____

4. What did Peter do besides praying for this man?

3:7 _____

Prayer and effort is the combination for saving men. The hand of compassion, however, is powerless unless extended in the name of Jesus Christ.

5. How complete was the cure?

3:8 _____

6. What fivefold result of the miracle can you find in verses 8 and

9? _____

_____

_____

The crowning evidence of a real conversion is when enemies are compelled to admit its reality.

We now have Peter's second sermon, giving a threefold testimony to Christ:

a. Christ as the Substance of all genuine miracles (verses 12-17)
b. Christ as the Redeemer of all souls (verses 18-21)
c. Christ as the Accomplisher of all prophecies (verses 22-26)

7. To whom does the credit belong for this miracle?

3:12, 13 _____

8. Whom does Peter charge with the guilt of the death of Christ?

3:14, 15 _____

9. What three titles does Peter here give to Christ?

3:14, 15 _____

_____

There are three paradoxes in these verses:
a. Man's perverted and fatal choice.
b. Man's hate, bringing death to the Lord of life.
c. God's love, causing life to come by death.

10. What was the connecting link between the risen Christ and the healed man?

3:16 _____

11. Who can find salvation through Jesus Christ?

3:19 _____

It has often been taught that Peter was calling upon Israel for national repentance, in which case Jesus would have immediately returned to set up His kingdom upon earth. There is nothing in verse 19, however, about Israel as a nation. The words were to a group of individuals and the promise was "to all that are afar off." Verse 21 declares plainly that Jesus must remain in heaven until the times of restitution.

12. What two different "times" are specified here?

3:19, 21 _____

_____

The "time of refreshing" would be the immediate result of repentance and faith. This undoubtedly refers to fullness of blessing to be possessed under the dispensation of the Holy Spirit.

13. What did Moses foresee for those who would reject Christ?

3:23 _____

Verses 20-23 simply enforce the exhortation to repentance by an appeal to the second coming of Christ. The early church lived and labored in expectation of this event. Note also that the Greek word for *times* in verse 19 is not the same as that used in verse 21. The first means seasons of refreshing as an immediate prospect. The second means a time of rest as a more remote prospect.

14. What was the message of the risen Christ to the Jews?

3:26 _____

Peter here tells us plainly, what the Jews as a people had overlooked, that the main blessing of their Abrahamic covenant was turning men away from their sins, not restored temporal power.

The Apostles Persecuted—Acts 4

"Behold their threatenings"

15. What happened when the Word seemed to be entering hearts?

4:1, 2 _____

16. What part of Peter's message particularly bothered the Sadducees?

4:2 _____

God moves in mysterious ways. One would think He would have stayed the hand of the adversary until Peter was through preaching. However, He knows how to make the wrath of man to praise Him.

17. What was the response to Peter's second sermon?

4:4 _____

18. What help did Peter receive in his answer to the council?

4:8 _____

19. Who was really behind the miracle that had been performed?

4:10 _____

Peter by himself had proved to be a straw blown by the wind, but Peter "filled with the Holy Ghost" was a mighty man of war, eloquent with heaven's thunder.

20. Who had previously told these leaders about the stone rejected by the builders?

MATTHEW 21:42 _____

21. What is the only name by which a man can be saved?

ACTS 4:12 _____

22. What was the only possible explanation for Peter's and John's conduct?

4:13 _____

16

Companionship with Jesus has made many an ordinary man extraordinary. Many a modern critic has "marveled" at the spiritual power of supposedly ignorant men. The word rendered *ignorant* means "private persons"—that is, holding no office, laymen.

23. What was the argument these critics could not get around?

4:14 _____

24. What was commendable in the man who had been healed?

4:14 _____

Christianity rests upon facts, not opinions. Put up a redeemed man and the mob cannot explain him. It is well when a preacher can carry his samples along with him. The church needs "Johnnie-on-the-spot" men—men who will be on hand when their testimony is worth something.

25. What besides the apostles' miracle working bothered the authorities?

4:18 _____

It is a big service to the devil when a preacher can be silenced. Men are ever seeking to silence the Word that convicts them. Work miracles by whatever power you please, men will say, but keep quiet about the saving name of Jesus Christ.

26. Whom did Peter propose to obey?

4:19 _____

27. What was the only thing that could be done with Peter and John?

4:21 _____

The church needs men who will stand by the colors, and not by their silence deny their Master, stealing away from the fight like cowards.

28. What did the Christians do about this persecution?

4:24 _____

29. How did the prayer meeting culminate?

4:31 _____

30. What was the fruit of their being "filled with the Holy Spirit"?

4:31 _____

Having all things in common was a spiritual movement, and was the expression of a high spiritual state. Such a plan could work only under these peculiar conditions. The plan lasted but a short time and evidently was not tried elsewhere. Hypocrites and self-seekers spoiled the plan.

Ananias and Sapphira—Acts 5

"Ye have agreed . . . to tempt the Spirit of the Lord"

The division of the book of Acts into chapters hinders the casual reader from noticing at this point that the action of Ananias and Sapphira is in contrast with that of Barnabas.

31. Who put the evil idea into the heart of Ananias?

5:3 _____

32. Who made a traitor out of one of the twelve?

LUKE 22:3 _____

33. What did Peter see cropping out in the early church?

II PETER 2:3 _____

34. In what way did Eve manifest covetousness in Eden?

GENESIS 3:6 _____

18

35. What was the first sin in the promised land?

JOSHUA 7:21 _____

Peter had spiritual insight to discover immediately that this was a Satanic attempt to injure the testimony of the church.

36. What was the sin of Ananias?

ACTS 5:4 _____

37. Against whom was the sin of Ananias?

5:4 _____

It is a striking fact that the first recorded funeral in the early church was a double one, and of hypocrites. It seems a severe penalty, but it should be remembered that when such events occur, it is to impart a clear warning when it is most needed.

38. What was the serious feature of their sin?

5:9 _____

Their position was an especially awful one, for they had been brought into closest contact with the powers of the world to come. The Holy Spirit had been manifested in a manner we know little of now. It was in such an atmosphere that these two people trifled. The Holy Spirit vindicated His authority. He is not only the Spirit of love, but the Spirit of truth. Deception in the name of the Holy Ghost needed to suffer a decisive blow at the outset.

39. What was the ultimate result to the church?

5:14 _____

There is too much of Ananias and Sapphira in all of us. It is easy to make it appear to others that we have done all we can, when we lie and know it. The danger is not so much that we do not give more, as in professing more than we practice. God wants true consecration and cannot be fooled.

40. How was the power of God publicly manifested?

5:16 _____

41. Who were offended by the growing influence of the apostles?

5:17 _____

42. Who let the apostles out of jail?

5:19 _____

43. What message were the apostles to proclaim?

5:20 _____

44. What did the apostles do after their escape?

5:25 _____

The bright spot in the picture is the fact that the common people favored the apostles. Their burning zeal for the salvation of souls won many. This was in contrast with the utter lack of care for souls on the part of the critics. That is still the difference between critics and true servants of God.

45. What is our best answer when men try to silence our testimony?

5:29 _____

46. What truth was Peter careful to emphasize?

5:30 _____

47. Why was Jesus "hanged on a tree" ?

I PETER 2:24 _____

48. What advice did Gamaliel give?

ACTS 5:35 _____

Caution is always commendable in moving against any religious activity. Be sure of your ground. Be tolerant toward those who are misled.

49. What will happen to a work if it is of men?

5:38 _____

50. What will happen to a work if it is of God?

5:39 _____

Gamaliel reasoned that their responsibility was discharged by simply letting the apostles alone. It was the leaders' business, however, to find out if these men were teaching God's truth, and if they were right, to side with them. If proved wrong, the leaders should warn against them. Gamaliel's doctrine is an easy one for spineless Christians.

51. What did the apostles decide to do?

5:42 _____

52. What was the apostles' glory?

GALATIANS 6:14 _____

check-up time No. 2

You have just studied some important truths about Acts 3–5. Review your study by rereading the questions and your written answers. If you aren't sure of an answer, reread the Scripture portion given to see if you can find the answer. Then take this test to see how well you understand important truths you have studied.

In the right-hand margin write "True" or "False" after each of the following statements.

1. Peter and John gave the lame man alms.   _____

2. The lame man praised God for his healing.   _____

3. The coming of Christ will fulfill many prophecies. _____

4. The Sadducees were glad to hear of the resurrection. _____

5. There is salvation only in the name of Jesus.   _____

6. Peter and John agreed to cease their preaching.   _____

7. The early Christians shared their material goods.   _____

8. Ananias and Sapphira gave all they had to the Lord. _____

9. An earthquake opened the prison doors for the apostles.   _____

10. Upon the advice of Gamaliel the apostles were set free.   _____

Turn to page 96 and check your answers.

The Church in Organization

Acts 6

The First Deacon—Acts 6

"Among you seven men"

1. What faction in the church started discord against the Hebrew Christians?

6:1 _____

2. What were the seven appointed men to do?

6:3 _____

The "tables" referred to were the counters at which money was distributed. The apostles were not depreciating the work of serving tables, but realized that those called to a special ministry should let such work be handled by others. D. L. Moody said he would rather set ten men to work than try to do ten men's work.

3. What were the qualifications for a deacon?

6:3 _____

4. What was the ministry of the apostles?

6:4 _____

Note that these seven men are not, in this chapter, called deacons, although those who later assumed this work in the church were called by that title. However, the word *ministration* in verse 1 is the Greek word *diakonia* and from it the word *deacon* is derived.

5. Who were the first two deacons named?

6:5 _____

The church should give the Holy Spirit men He can control. The first two named probably influenced the spiritual life and history of the church more than any other men outside of Peter and Paul. Deacons may have an influence world-wide.

6. Who became the first martyr of the church?

ACTS 7:57-59 _____

7. Who became the first lay evangelist of the church?

ACTS 8:5 _____

The word *deacon* means primarily "errand runner." The deacons were the practical servants of the church (I TIMOTHY 3:8-12). They attended to benevolences, and did house-to-house visitation and personal work.

8. Who were among the converts to the church?

ACTS 6:7 _____

We find in the New Testament no warrant for ecclesiastical grades in the ministry of the churches—an ascending series of rulers to govern churches, merged into one great federation. To each local church was committed the management of its own affairs; each endowed with authority to perform every function necessary to a church. While each church was independent, co-operative relations were entered into (ROMANS 15:26, 27; GALATIANS 2:10).

9. What kind of reputation did Stephen have?

6:8 _____.__

The name of *Stephen* means "crown." He was the first to receive a martyr crown.

10. What was there about his work that the people could not get around?

6:10 _____

11. What had Jesus promised to those who should be yielded to His Spirit?

LUKE 21:15 _____

12. What did the men who were so zealous for the law of God do?

ACTS 6:12 _____

The word *suborned* (verse 11) means "provided." In other words, they bribed men to be witnesses.

13. Bribed witnesses also perverted the statements of what man?

MATTHEW 26:59-61 _____

14. What happened while they were accusing Stephen of blaspheming Moses?

ACTS 6:15 _____

15. Of what should this have reminded them?

EXODUS 34:29 _____

Note that Stephen was possessed by a holy calm even when grossly misrepresented. Calmness is usually the sign of a great man. The little man loses his head. God has a way of putting a certain light upon the faces of Spirit-filled men which cannot be mistaken.

check-up time No. 3

You have just studied some important truths about Acts 6. Review your study by rereading the questions and your written answers. If you aren't sure of an answer, reread the Scripture portion given to see if you can find the answer. Then take this test to see how well you understand important truths you have studied.

In the right-hand margin write "True" or "False" after each of the following statements.

1. The Hebrew widows were being cared for by the church. _____

2. The seven deacons were to be men full of the Holy Ghost. _____

3. The apostles wanted to give themselves to prayer and the ministry of the Word. _____

4. Many more disciples joined the early church. _____

5. There were many priests converted. _____

6. Stephen was able to speak with great wisdom. _____

7. Many witnesses spoke the truth against Stephen. _____

8. Stephen was accused of blaspheming against the temple. _____

9. Stephen's persecutors were Gentiles. _____

10. Stephen's face revealed his true faith. _____

Turn to page 96 and check your answers.

The Church in Expansion

ACTS 7, 8

A Martyr Expounding—Acts 7

"I see the heavens opened"

Stephen is one of the most beautiful characters in the Bible. The fact that he was full of grace and power led him through a great, but short, ministry like that of John the Baptist.

We have the story of but one day of his life—the last one. What a remarkable picture it is! Stephen stood at the parting of the ways. He was a transition from Peter to Paul.

1. How far back did Stephen begin the history of the Hebrews?

7:2 _____

2. To what point in history did he lead?

7:8 _____

3. What was the outcome of Joseph's being left in a pit to die?

7:11-13 _____

4. What was the result of Jesus' being left in a tomb?

ROMANS 1:4 _____

5. How did God preserve the Messianic seed?

ACTS 7:21 _____

6. How did God equip Moses to serve Him?

7:22 _____

7. Instead of leading Israel, what was Moses compelled to do?

7:29 _____

8. How did God appear to Moses in the wilderness?

7:30 _____

9. What purpose did God have for Moses' life?

7:35 _____

10. What was Israel's spiritual condition in the wilderness?

7:41 _____

11. What had been the attitude of Israel in those days?

7:51 _____

12. Who had brought a similar charge against Israel?

MATTHEW 23:37, 38 _____

At first reading, Stephen's sermon seems disconnected, but carefully studied, we find Old Testament quotations used with rare skill. He proved that the Christ they murdered was the One their prophets had foretold. He summed up their history, revealing their hardness of heart, spiritual deafness and continuous resistance of the Holy Spirit, down to the very council before whom he was speaking.

13. Who was the One whom they had crucified?

ACTS 7:52 _____

14. What encouragement was given to Stephen at this point?

7:55 _____

15. What is the reason men still stop their ears?

JOHN 3:19, 20 _____

ACTS 7:58 is the first mention of Saul. He was apparently a delighted spectator. The loud voice of Stephen's prayer, however, never ceased to ring in his ears. Perhaps but for that audible prayer, the church would not have had a Paul.

16. Who soon took Stephen's place as a mighty witness?

ACTS 9:19, 20 _____

17. What were Stephen's last words about his murderers?

ACTS 7:60 _____

18. With whom may Stephen be compared?

LUKE 23:34 _____

With the murder of Stephen the Jewish leaders seemed to have carried the day. But had they? Time alone could reveal God's larger plan. He makes no mistakes. The world had been shown how a Christian could die. The violent hand of the persecutor became like the scattering hand of a sower, and the gospel seed sprouted wherever it fell.

An Evangelist Witnessing—Acts 8

"Preached unto him Jesus"

19. What did these Christian laymen do?

8:4 _____

20. What accompanied the preaching of Philip?

8:6 _____

21. What rival did Philip have?

8:9 _____

Be sure to notice that while it is stated that Simon "believed," he was "wonderstruck." Emphasis is laid on his incapacity to understand the nature and character of Christian truth. It is doubtful if his belief had gotten below his collar.

22. What special message was needed by Christians in Samaria?

8:14, 15 _____

23. Since these people had believed on Jesus, what must they have received in some sense?

ACTS 2:38, 39; JOHN 7:37-39 _____

It is clear from the record that at this early period, as each new part of the divine commission was carried out (ACTS 1:8), special manifestations of the Spirit awaited the presence of some of the apostles, and the laying on of hands.

24. What proved that Simon's belief was only a head knowledge?

ACTS 8:18 _____

25. While his head belief was all right, what was wrong?

8:21 _____

26. What kind of knowledge will save a sinner?

ROMANS 10:9 _____

The word *thought* in verse 22 means "mature plan." He had his mind filled with a monetary scheme.

27. In the midst of successful work, what was Philip told to do?

ACTS 8:26 _____

28. What indicates the Ethiopian was a seeker of truth?

8:28 _____

30

The word *join* in verse 29 means "glue thyself to him." To get next to a man and warm up to him is the first step in personal work.

29. What Scripture passage is good for personal work?

8:32 _____

30. What confession of faith did the eunuch make?

8:37 _____

31. What followed the man's confession of faith?

8:38 _____

32. Brought together by an angel, how were these two men parted?

8:39 _____

Tradition tells us that the eunuch labored to evangelize his countrymen. We never can tell what may be the result of winning one soul.

You have just studied some important truths about Acts 7, 8. Review your study by rereading the questions and your written answers. If you aren't sure of an answer, reread the Scripture portion given to see if you can find the answer. Then take this test to see how well you understand important truths you have studied.

In the right-hand margin write "True" or "False" after each of the following statements.

1. God promised to give Palestine to Abraham as an inheritance.   _____

2. The Israelites accepted Moses as their leader after he had slain the Egyptian.   _____

3. God sent Moses back to Egypt to be a ruler over the Israelites.   _____

4. The Israelites continued to worship God in the wilderness.   _____

5. Stephen saw a vision of Christ in heaven.   _____

6. Philip had a good evangelistic ministry in Samaria. _____

7. Simon was a sorcerer that bewitched the people.   _____

8. Simon wanted to buy the power of the Holy Ghost with money.   _____

9. The Ethiopian eunuch was reading from the book of Psalms.   _____

10. After the eunuch received Christ he was baptized. _____

Turn to page 96 and check your answers.

The Church
in Dispersion

ACTS 9–12

A Jew Converted—Acts 9

"He is a chosen vessel"

The abrupt introduction, "Saul, yet breathing out threatenings," is deeply suggestive. It reveals Saul as a man of intense energy, with a soul on fire to do one thing.

1. Where was Saul when a light from heaven came to him?

9:3 _____

2. The supernatural light came at what time of day?

26:13; 22:6 _____

This hour was chosen in order that the glory of this heaven-sent light should not be confounded with any natural phenomena. Critics say it was a sunstroke. Dr. Parker answers: "Look at Saul before his sunstroke—snorting, blaspheming, persecuting. Look at him while he is having it—he prayeth. Look at him when he was out of it—saint, hero, missionary, martyr." May such "sunstrokes" afflict the whole church!

3. Who was Saul really persecuting?

9:4 _____

4. What did Jesus tell Saul he was kicking against?

9:5 _____

Pricks refer to goads used on oxen. When an ox kicks, he drives the goad into himself. No man can rave against Christianity and be a happy man.

5. Is salvation based on my "good works" or are my "good works" a result of my salvation?

Ephesians 2:10 _____

6. What happened when Saul received strength from the right source?

Acts 9:22 _____

7. What was Saul doing during his time of blindness?

9:11 _____

The breath of rage had been turned to the breath of prayer. Such a change must be accounted for. This is precisely what Christianity does in men. It makes the lion lie down with the lamb.

8. Why was Ananias to proceed at once to Saul?

9:15 _____

9. To what three classes was Paul destined to preach?

9:15 _____

Thus did Jesus Christ lay hold of the devil's most enthusiastic servant, the chief enemy of the gospel, and one of the finest intellects of the day.

10. What special thing did the Lord desire to reveal?

9:16 _____

11. What did Saul need in addition to natural sight?

9:17 _____

45. How coul(

PSALM 4:8 ___

46. How lon
prayers for P(

ACTS 12:6 __

God often del
Peter was ma
hour and then

47. What pro

PSALM 34:7

48. What ins
Peter out?

ACTS 12:8 _

Omnipotence
We will mak
His.

49. How lor

12:10 ___

There is alw
us what we

50. What k:

12:12 ___

51. What v

12:12 ___

12. What message did he start preaching at once?

9:20 _____

Findlay says: "The conversion of Paul is a psychological and ethical problem that cannot be accounted for save by Paul's own interpretation of the change wrought in him. He saw Jesus and surrendered to Him." No soul is beyond the reach of the same divine grace. The need of our day is not a new gospel but the gospel anew.

13. What was the purpose in the healing of Aeneas?

9:35 _____

14. For what was Dorcas of Joppa noted?

9:36 _____

15. What is a sure mark of Christian discipleship?

JOHN 15:8 _____

16. What was the Lord's purpose in this miracle?

ACTS 9:42 _____

A Gentile Accepted—Acts 10, 11

"Granted repentance unto life"

Caesarea was the seat of the Roman governors, named from the Roman Caesar. A military stronghold and naval arsenal, it was the last place one might expect to find a man who desired to be a Christian.

17. What type of man was Cornelius?

10:2 _____

18. How was God preparing Peter to meet Cornelius' need?

10:9 _____

35

38. Wh

11:22

39. Wh:

11:23

Notice
with Je:
fore me

40. Wh

11:26

A Pr

"His ch

41. Wh

12:2

42. Wh

12:3

43. Wh

12:4

44. To

12:5

The we
with g
hangin

The Church in Missions

Acts 13, 14

PAUL'S FIRST MISSIONARY JOURNEY

A Journey Started—Acts 13

"They sent them away"

1. What two men were called by the Spirit for leadership?

13:2 _____

2. What was Paul's preparation for this work?

Acts 11:23-26; Galatians 1:18 _____

_____

3. What did the ordination council do before sending them forth?

Acts 13:3 _____

4. Who sent them on their way?

13:4 _____

This is the beginning of a great forward step—the first time the gospel went to sea.

5. Who disputed the field with them?

13:6 _____

42

6. *Bar-jesus* means "son of Saviour." Whose child did Saul call him?

13:10 _____

7. What judgment was pronounced upon the trifler?

13:11 _____

Paul began with the sorcerer where the Lord had begun with him. Blindness had given him a chance to think.

8. What was the desire of the public Official who was with Bar-jesus?

13:7 _____

9. What was the official's reaction to Paul's doctrine?

13:12 _____

Note: The name *Paul* (verse 9) was the nearest Latin equivalent of the Jewish name "Saul." It means "little." (Saul means "desired one.") The new name may have been suggested by Paul's littleness of stature. However, there may have been spiritual reasons for the change. Paul refers to himself as "less than the least of all saints"—"the least of the apostles."

10. What was John Mark's reaction to the trip?

13:13 _____

11. What two classes did Paul perceive to be present in the synagogue at Antioch in Pisidia?

13:16 _____

12. How did Paul present the Lord Jesus?

13:28, 29 _____

13. How did God manifest His power in Christ?

13:30 _____

14. What was the promise to all who would truly believe?

13:39 _____

Justified means "reckoned righteous," or made as though one had never sinned.

15. What is the result of justification?

ROMANS 5:1 _____

16. What was the only attraction needed to draw a crowd?

ACTS 13:44 _____

17. How far did the Jews go in their manifestation of envy?

13:45 _____

18. What did the Jews forfeit in their rejection of Christ?

13:46 _____

Note at this point that it was not the offer of a temporal kingdom which the Jews had despised, but the offer of everlasting life through the gospel—the same offer that was later made to all nations.

19. What is the place of the Jew so far as the gospel is concerned?

ROMANS 10:1-13 _____

20. How many of the Gentiles received eternal life?

ACTS 13:48 _____

Ordination signifies the divine inclining of these Gentiles toward salvation. Even though it is by the Father's "drawing" (JOHN 6:44) that men are disposed to accept the gospel, this does not annul or counteract man's own agency. Others who did not believe, could have believed if they had wanted to. If men are lost, it is the result of their own decision. God in His foreknowledge (ROMANS 8:29) knows who will accept, so it is His determination in unison with man's choice that brings about salvation.

False Worship Rejected—Acts 14

"We also are men"

21. Why were so many converted in the synagogue?

14:1 _____

There is a great difference in the way words are spoken. They may be so spoken from the heart and warmed by the Spirit that conviction will be brought to hearts.

22. What definition of the gospel do you find here?

14:3 _____

23. How was the gospel confirmed at the beginning?

14:3 _____

24. What made the cripple at Lystra an apparently hopeless case?

14:8 _____

25. What did Paul perceive about the crippled man?

14:9 _____

26. Who is the author of faith?

HEBREWS 12:2 _____

27. What did the crowd think of the healing?

ACTS 14:11 _____

28. How far did they carry this idea?

14:13 _____

Their action reveals the longing in the human mind for the manifestation of Deity in human form. The doctrine of the incarnation is by no means contrary to the intuitive conceptions of the human mind.

29. How did Barnabas and Paul guard the honor of Christ?

14:14 _____

30. Why did they refuse to have people bow down to them?

14:15 _____

The love of the applause of the religious world is a deadly thing. Some preachers are not so ready to turn all attention away from themselves.

31. How has God manifested Himself to those without the Scriptures?

14:17 _____

32. What did the people finally do to Paul?

14:19 _____

33. For what purpose did Paul and Barnabas return to Iconium and Antioch?

14:22 _____

Evangelistic work is important, but there must be pastoral work and Bible teaching to preserve the fruit.

34. What is in store for the Christian in this life?

14:22 _____

35. What should we be willing to bear for Christ's sake?

ROMANS 8:17 _____

36. What officers were appointed as permanent directors of the spiritual affairs of the church?

ACTS 14:23 _____

37. What was the striking thing in their report?

14:27 _____

38. To whom did they give all the glory for successes?

14:27 _____

check-up time No. 6

You have just studied some important truths about Acts 13, 14. Review your study by rereading the questions and your written answers. If you aren't sure of an answer, reread the Scripture portion given to see if you can find the answer. Then take this test to see how well you understand important truths you have studied.

In the right-hand margin write "True" or "False" after each of the following statements.

1. The Holy Spirit sent Paul and Barnabas on their first missionary journey. _____

2. The deputy followed Elymas the sorcerer instead of the apostle Paul. _____

3. From David's seed God raised up a Saviour. _____

4. The Gentiles desired to hear the gospel message more than the Jews. _____

5. Almost the whole city of Antioch came to hear the Word of God preached. _____

6. The apostles were discouraged at the persecution. _____

7. Paul healed a crippled man who had never walked. _____

8. The Jews put Paul in prison at Lystra. _____

9. Paul and Barnabas ordained elders in the churches. _____

10. Paul felt that God had closed the door of faith to the Gentiles. _____

Turn to page 96 and check your answers.

The Church in Conference

ACTS 15

The Jerusalem Decision—Acts 15

"Came together for to consider"

This is one of the most important chapters in ecclesiastical history. A wrong step at the council of churches in Jerusalem and Christian liberty in Christ would have been lost and Christianity would have become a Jewish sect.

1. Who brought in confusing teachings concerning law and grace?

15:1 _____

2. Who instantly and sharply resisted their teaching?

15:2 _____

3. What if circumcision were made necessary to salvation?

GALATIANS 5:3 _____

4. What vital fact was in contradiction to making any part of the law essential to salvation?

ROMANS 10:4 _____

5. What mystery was Paul the first to understand?

EPHESIANS 3:3-6 _____

6. What occurred when Gentiles received Jesus Christ?

Acts 15:8 _____

Here is a fine argument. God had settled the law question by undeniably placing the seal of the Holy Spirit upon those who were entirely uninstructed in the Mosaic law. The law had not been preached to the Gentiles.

7. What were these mistaken teachers doing by dictating the terms of salvation?

15:10 _____

8. What was the "good news," both for Jew and Gentile?

15:11 _____

9. How was it shown that the law is without power to save?

Galatians 2:21 _____

10. What is God's program for the age of grace?

Acts 15:14 _____

11. What does the second coming of Christ await?

Romans 11:25 _____

12. What is our work in this present age?

Luke 14:23 _____

13. How will God deal with the Jewish nation?

Romans 11:25, 26 _____

14. What was the proposed settlement of the dispute at Antioch?

Acts 15:22, 23 _____

15. Of whose guidance were they sure in the church council?

15:28 _____

Later, Peter's old trait of cowardice cropped out (GALATIANS 2:11-18), leading him to forget his own words in the Jerusalem council and to disregard their decision. To gratify the prejudice of influential Jews, he withdrew from the Gentiles and caused others also to do likewise. Paul charged them all with lack of backbone and with promoting a divisive spirit at a critical time. The rebuke proved effectual. These temporary defections cropping out in the lives of great leaders often puzzle us. We need to be reminded that ministers are human, and that even the most active workers need our constant prayers.

16. What painful incident occurred just prior to Paul's missionary journey?

15:39 _____

17. Why was Barnabas more lenient toward Mark (Marcus)?

COLOSSIANS 4:10 _____

18. Was Barnabas' confidence in Mark later rewarded?

II TIMOTHY 4:11 _____

19. May God have had a purpose in breaking up Paul and Barnabas?

ROMANS 8:28 _____

Paul's distrust of Mark may have helped to brace up Mark. There are some modern Marks who need "jacking up." They have no respect for their engagements. Both Paul and Barnabas were wrong in exhibiting temper and in not trying to understand each other's viewpoint. Christian workers often become overwrought.

20. Where did Barnabas and Mark go to minister?

ACTS 15:39 _____

21. Where did Paul and Silas go to minister?

15:41 _____

22. How many evangelistic parties went forth?

15:39, 40 _____

check-up time No. 7

You have just studied some important truths about Acts 15. Review your study by rereading the questions and your written answers. If you aren't sure of an answer, reread the Scripture portion given to see if you can find the answer. Then take this test to see how well you understand important truths you have studied.

In the right-hand margin write "True" or "False" after each of the following statements.

1. The first church council was over the problem of the mode of baptism. _____

2. The council was held in the city of Rome. _____

3. Paul was allowed to tell of his ministry. _____

4. Peter presided at the first church council. _____

5. The council said the Gentile Christians were not to be burdened with the ritual of circumcision. _____

6. The Holy Ghost guided the men in their decision. _____

7. The decision of the council was rejected. _____

8. Paul was happy to receive Mark as a co-laborer. _____

9. Barnabas and Paul formed two evangelistic teams instead of one. _____

10. Barnabas and Mark ministered in Jerusalem. _____

Turn to page 96 and check your answers.

The Church in Extension

ACTS 16–18

PAUL'S SECOND MISSIONARY JOURNEY

Three Converts Won—Acts 16

"What must I do?"

1. What young man with great possibilities did Paul meet?

16:1 _____

2. Why did Paul want Timothy to be circumcised?

16:3 _____

3. What did Paul do in the case of Titus?

GALATIANS 2:3-5 _____

It was not a compromise of principle to have Timothy circumcised. Paul clearly taught that this rite was not essential. Timothy, being part Jew, could have access to the synagogues to preach Christ if he was circumcised according to the law. Furthermore, the fact that his father was a Greek would raise a question about him, unless it was known that he had been circumcised.

Titus, on the other hand, was a Greek, heathen-born. Those who demanded his circumcision did it upon the ground that a Gentile must become a Jew before he could be a Christian, making it essential to salvation.

4. In order to win men to Christ, how far would Paul go?

I Corinthians 9:22 _____

_____

In the case of Titus, Paul was intolerant in the defense of vital principles. In Timothy's case he was willing to be tolerant of Jewish prejudices in order to win them to Christ.

5. How were their steps ordered of the Lord?

Acts 16:6 _____

6. Against what other place were they warned?

16:7 _____

We may need the Spirit's guidance to prevent our preaching.

7. To what place were they called through a night vision?

16:9 _____

8. What were they called to do through that vision?

16:10 _____

9. What happened at the meeting on the river bank?

16:13, 14 _____

_____

10. What should we do if we wish to profit by the preaching of the gospel?

Psalm 119:18 _____

11. What did the girl soothsayer say about Paul and Silas?

Acts 16:17 _____

_____

12. What is the only "spirit" the Christian should consult?

John 16:13 _____

13. In what name alone may demon-possessed people be delivered?

Acts 16:18 _____

14. What was the reason for antagonism against the gospel?

16:19 _____

15. What was done with Paul and Silas?

16:23 _____

16. How did God vindicate His servants?

16:26 _____

In the same chapter of the New Testament we have the record of two remarkable conversions: Lydia, on a quiet river bank, finds Christ through the gentle opening of her heart by the Spirit. The jailer, in the midst of the commotion of an earthquake, is born again. Whether cultured lady or tough turnkey, the need for Christ is the same.

17. What is the complete answer to the salvation question?

16:31 _____

18. What does a man do to be lost?

John 3:18, 36 _____

19. What evidence is there that the jailer was saved?

16:34 _____

56

When you were born again, did you have a desire to wash the stripes you cruelly inflicted before you were saved? Could you forget the lives you had injured and the graves you had dug for others? Real salvation drives a man back to his past.

20. What did the magistrates desire to do with their prisoners?

16:35 _____

21. Why did Paul refuse to be brushed aside so easily?

16:37 _____

_____

The Philosophers Come—Acts 17
"We will hear thee again"

Paul's two epistles to the Thessalonians (the first two letters he wrote) give such a glowing picture of the Thessalonian church that it is interesting to meet here the account of its founding.

22. On what did Paul base his reasoning in the synagogue in Thessalonica?

17:2 _____

23. What did Paul "open" to them?

17:3 _____

24. What did Paul prove to them?

17:3 _____

Types, shadows, prophecies and express declarations of the Old Testament, all harmoniously converge upon one momentous necessity: *"He must needs* have suffered." God had no other plan (I PETER 1:11).

25. What did the enemies give the evangelists credit for doing?

17:6 _____

26. What kind of charge was lodged against them?

17:7 _____

27. What had been the daily habit of the Jews in Berea?

17:11 _____

28. What will a real seeker for truth always do?

JOHN 5:39 _____

29. What happened when they tested the preaching by the Word?

ACTS 17:12 _____

30. What two schools of philosophy were encountered?

17:18 _____

They were the materialists and the moralists of that day. Epicurus taught that the great end of existence was enjoyment; creation was ascribed to chance. The Stoics were pantheists and held that providence was governed by fatal necessity.

31. What was Paul's statement concerning them?

17:22 _____

Superstitious should read "religious." They admitted everything that came in the dress of religion, but in it all, there was no knowledge of God.

32. How did Paul knock the props from under their philosophies?

17:24 _____

33. What does the creature depend upon God to provide?

17:25 _____

58

34. How were the conceited Athenians compared to others?

17:26 _____

35. Who is back of all the movements of men?

Daniel 2:20, 21 _____

36. What did Paul say about finding the true God?

Acts 17:27 _____

37. What "modernistic" writers did Paul quote?

17:28 _____

38. What should common sense teach every man?

17:29 _____

39. What attitude has God taken toward the world's ignorance?

17:30 _____

Winked at is more literally "forebore," that is, God allowed it to pass without special interference (not that man's guilt was excused).

40. What does God demand of all men?

17:30 _____

41. What happens if men do not repent?

17:31 _____

42. What is the only way to escape judgment?

John 5:24 _____

43. What will be the basis of judgment?

John 12:48 _____

A Journey Done—Acts 18

"I will return"

Corinth claims distinction as the residence of the apostle during his most critical contest for the faith. There he wrote his first apostolic letters (Thessalonians). To the saints at Corinth he addressed two epistles. From Corinth, on this second visit, he wrote his most elaborate epistle—Romans.

44. What determination did Paul make as he entered Corinth?

I Corinthians 2:1, 2 _____

45. What friends did Paul find at Corinth?

Acts 18:2 _____

46. How did God provide for Paul's personal needs in Corinth?

18:3 _____

47. What made Paul a convincing speaker?

18:5 _____

48. What is the only alternative if men refuse the gospel?

18:6 _____

49. What responsibility rests upon Christians?

Ezekiel 33:9 _____

50. Who came under Paul's influence and was converted?

Acts 18:8 _____

51. What statement of Jesus was reaffirmed to Paul (Matthew 28:18-20)?

18:10 _____

52. Why did Paul shave his head and take his vow (18:18)?

NUMBERS 6:1-21 _____

Paul did not believe that carrying out a practice enjoined under the law contributed anything to salvation. Why did he take this Nazarite vow? Simply to maintain hard discipline over himself. The man to look out for is the one who is rigid on others and easy on himself.

53. Why would Paul not remain in Ephesus at that time?

ACTS 18:21 _____

It was customary for a man whose hair had grown long under a vow to take the hair to Jerusalem to burn. The apostle of the gospel of liberty evidently carried his hair to Jerusalem, according to the Levitical law.

54. What did Paul do after visiting Jerusalem?

18:23 _____

55. What were some of the gifts of Apollos?

18:24 _____

56. What instruction did Apollos lack?

18:25 _____

57. Who imparted to him the truth he needed to know?

18:26 _____

58. What was the result of the personal work of Aquila and Priscilla?

18:27, 28 _____

check-up time No. 8

You have just studied some important truths about Acts 16–18. Review your study by rereading the questions and your written answers. If you aren't sure of an answer, reread the Scripture portion given to see if you can find the answer. Then take this test to see how well you understand important truths you have studied.

In the right-hand margin write "True" or "False" after each of the following statements.

1. Paul had Timothy circumcised because Timothy was part Jew and part Greek. _____

2. The Holy Ghost directed Paul's ministry into Asia. _____

3. Lydia was the first convert to the gospel in Europe. _____

4. The Philippian jailer believed and was saved. _____

5. The Jews of Berea rejected the Word of God. _____

6. Paul preached on Mars' hill in the city of Athens. _____

7. The people of Athens readily received the gospel. _____

8. Paul supported himself with his fishing skill. _____

9. Paul stayed at Corinth only a few days. _____

10. Apollos was an eloquent man, mighty in the Scriptures. _____

Turn to page 96 and check your answers.

The Churches Revisited

ACTS 19, 20

PAUL'S THIRD MISSIONARY JOURNEY

Ephesian Opposition—Acts 19

"Our craft is in danger"

1. What was lacking in the experience of Ephesian believers?

19:3 _____

2. What question did Paul ask them?

19:2 _____

Note the A.S.V.: "Did ye receive . . . *when* ye believed?" It was not a question of whether they received the Spirit at some time subsequent to believing, but whether on the occasion of believing they received the Spirit's witness.

3. What had John the Baptist said about the Holy Ghost?

MATTHEW 3:11 _____

Note the last phrase of verse 2 in A.S.V. "We did not so much as hear whether the Holy Ghost was given." Of the existence of the Holy Spirit no disciple of John could be ignorant. But John died before the Holy Spirit was given, and likewise these disciples were unacquainted with the happenings at Pentecost.

4. What baptism did they then accept?

Acts 19:5 _____

John's baptism was a washing symbolical of repentance which he preached in preparation for Christ's appearance. Baptism into the name of Christ was the outward seal of having been saved through the death and resurrection of Christ (Romans 6:4).

5. What was the formula for baptism given by Jesus?

Matthew 28:19 _____

_____

Observe that this was a peculiar circumstance. These were Jewish proselytes looking forward to the coming of the Messiah, not knowing that He had come and gone. There is no warrant here for changing the baptismal formula for all believers.

6. What did Paul do when opposition became pronounced?

Acts 19:9 _____

7. What manifestation of divine power was given through Paul?

19:12 _____

This very unusual form of miracle was adapted to meet the superstitions of Ephesus. It refuted their magic arts, and the instant healings challenged comparisons. People did not even have to be present to be healed, and there were no long incantations.

8. What happened to men who had gotten into Christian work the wrong way?

19:14-16 _____

9. What was the effect of the lesson taught these triflers?

19:17 _____

10. How did God turn the instance to good?

19:18 _____

11. Why did the craftsmen get concerned about religion?

19:24-27 _____

12. What was the result of this uproar?

19:29 _____

13. What did the people do in their zeal for idol worship?

19:32 _____

14. Who put a stop to the racket?

19:35 _____

15. What course was open if the craftsmen had complaints?

19:38 _____

16. Why did the town clerk stop the uproar?

19:40; 21:31 _____

Ephesian Consolation—Acts 20
"I commend you to God"

Three years of faithful effort had been given Ephesus and the surrounding region. Many churches had been planted, possibly the seven addressed in the book of Revelation. Paul's first epistle to the Corinthians had been written.

17. What took place on the first day of the week?

20:7 _____

18. What was the probable cause of the young man's falling?

20:8, 9 _____

19. What did Paul do in the midst of his sermon?

20:10, 11 _____

20. What Old Testament story does Paul's action recall?

II KINGS 4:34 _____

21. What miracle by Peter is paralleled?

ACTS 9:36-40 _____

22. In what spirit had Paul served the churches?

ACTS 20:18, 19 _____

23. What two kinds of Christian work had he done?

20:20 _____

24. What was to be Paul's next move?

20:22 _____

25. What premonition did he have regarding this trip?

20:22 _____

26. How did Paul face the prospect of trouble?

20:24 _____

27. What was Paul's only ambition?

20:24 _____

28. What was he able to say in his last epistle?

II TIMOTHY 4:7 _____

29. What could Paul say as to the people of Ephesus?

ACTS 20:26 _____

30. What further could he say?

II CORINTHIANS 4:2 _____

31. What is every preacher expected to do?

JEREMIAH 26:2 _____

32. What duties did Paul define for elders?

ACTS 20:28 _____

Note that the elders (verse 17) are not called "overseers" (Greek—
episcopos, elsewhere translated "bishop"). An elder (meaning a mature
Christian) was, as to his official duties, a bishop or overseer of the
spiritual interests of the church. These were not two offices.

33. How has the Church been purchased?

20:28 _____

34. What conditions did Paul foresee in the Ephesian church?

20:29 _____

35. How was Paul's anticipation of the church fulfilled?

REVELATION 2:1, 4, 5 _____

36. To what did Paul commend the Ephesian elders on his de-
parture?

ACTS 20:32 _____

37. What is God's Word able to do for us?

20:32 _____

Remember that these believers had no New Testament such as we
have. The greater part was yet unwritten. All that was written was in
the form of letters held by distant churches. How much more securely
we may commend each other to the permanent record of divine revelation! Christian progress is impossible without it.

67

38. What special truth did Paul want them to know?

20:35 _____

_____

39. Why should we freely give?

MATTHEW 10:8 _____

40. What was Paul's Christian farewell?

ACTS 20:36 _____

There are no endearments so strong as those created by Christian fellowship. All other unions perish. All other associations are but for the passing moment. Perhaps no partings are so hard as those of the soul. One who has watched over souls is peculiarly endeared, for he has had fellowship with the inmost life of the people.

check-up time No. 9

You have just studied some important truths about
Acts 19–20. Review your study by rereading the
questions and your written answers. If you aren't
sure of an answer, reread the Scripture portion given
to see if you can find the answer. Then take this
test to see how well you understand important truths
you have studied.

In the right-hand margin write "True" or "False"
after each of the following statements.

1. In Ephesus Paul preached in the synagogue. _____

2. Paul preached in Ephesus two years. _____

3. The sons of Sceva healed the man with the evil
spirit. _____

4. Demetrius was a carpenter. _____

5. Most of the Ephesians worshiped Diana. _____

6. Eutychus fell out of the loft while Paul was preaching. _____

7. Paul said that the young man was dead. _____

8. Paul said farewell to the Ephesian elders at Miletus. _____

9. Paul felt that he must go to Jerusalem. _____

10. The Ephesian elders were happy to see Paul go. _____

Turn to page 96 and check your answers.

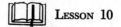

Paul in Jerusalem

ACTS 21–23

The Preacher Accused—Acts 21

"Away with him"

1. What warning did Paul receive from disciples at Tyre?

21:4 _____

The literal reading is "set foot in Jerusalem"—an imperative command.

2. What was the divine basis of this warning?

21:4 _____

3. What warning had Paul previously received?

20:22, 23 _____

_____

4. What did Paul himself admit after he reached Jerusalem?

22:17, 18 _____

Commentators have said that these exhortations not to go to Jerusalem were probably the voice of human affection only. This seems to be dodging plain words. Why attempt to make Paul a perfect man? We admit that Peter and others made mistakes.

5. What did Paul do about the warning?

21:5, 6 _____

6. What is meant by "one of the seven"?

21:8; cf. 6:5 _____

7. What divine gift did the four daughters possess?

21:9 _____

8. On what occasion had this been foretold?

2:18 _____

"Prophesying" here refers to divine inspiration to interpret or unfold the truth, not to foretell events.

9. What significant thing did Agabus the prophet do?

21:11 _____

_____

10. What shows that it was the voice of God speaking?

21:11 _____

11. Why was Paul not moved by prospects of death?

II Corinthians 11:23 _____

Commentators again come to the rescue and say Agabus did not forbid Paul but simply warned him of trouble ahead. But are not the best judges of what Agabus meant those who were present and who exhorted Paul not to go—that is, to avert unnecessary peril and to prolong his usefulness? Paul needed no one to tell him there was trouble ahead (20:22). The question is, Was it by God's absolute or His permissive will that Paul went to Jerusalem?

12. What did his friends say when Paul would not be dissuaded?

Acts 21:14 _____

13. On what work did Paul render a report?

21:19 _____

14. How was his report received?

21:20 _____

15. What scheme was proposed so the Jews would favor Paul?

21:22-24 _____

_____

This was, no doubt, well-meant but mistaken advice. It was perhaps not unlawful for Paul to enter upon ceremonial purification with these men who had taken a Nazarite vow (NUMBERS 6) and were entering the closing ceremony of seven days, but it was of doubtful policy. It would tend to confirm some Jews in the idea that Paul regarded the law essential. The act did not stop the criticism nor prevent the outbreak of hostility against him. Learn from it that good men may give bad advice and take false steps in defense of the gospel.

16. What was the result of this scheme?

21:27 _____

We are called upon to face some plain facts—the failure of Peter, the apostasy of Judas, the lying of Ananias and Sapphira, the failure of Mark, the quarrel between Paul and Barnabas, the doubtful compromise of Peter with the Jews. Need we fear to admit that Paul also mistook the mind of the Lord?

17. What charges did the Jews place against Paul?

21:28 _____

_____

18. Whom did they believe he had brought into the temple?

21:29 _____

19. What prevented his being immediately killed?

21:31, 32 _____

20. What was the cry of the mob?

21:36 _____

The Accused Is Protected—Acts 22

"This man is a Roman"

21. What caused the crowd now to give heed to Paul?

22:2 _____

22. What did Paul tell them under the guise of a "defense"?

22:3-21 _____

_____

23. What precipitated another outcry?

22:21, 22 _____

24. How did they express their contempt for one who would endeavor to save the Gentiles?

22:23 _____

25. How did the captain propose to get to the truth of the matter?

22:24 _____

26. What was the only thing that saved Paul at this time?

22:25 _____

27. Where is the Christian's real citizenship?

PHILIPPIANS 3:20 _____

28. How much weight did Paul's Roman citizenship have?

ACTS 22:26, 29 _____

_____

29. How had Paul procured this citizenship?

22:28 _____

30. What was done with him when his citizenship was established?

22:30 _____

The Conspiracy Detected—Acts 23

"Bound ourselves under a great curse"

Almost twenty-five years had elapsed since Paul had intensely endorsed this same council's persecution of Stephen.

31. Who had made a similar defense on this same spot?

ACTS 6:8–7:1 _____

32. Who else had stood there when Caiaphas pronounced a death sentence?

MATTHEW 26:57 _____

33. What was Paul's attitude on this occasion?

ACTS 23:1 _____

34. What was his attitude before he became a Christian?

PHILIPPIANS 3:6 _____

35. What was his attitude while persecuting Christians?

ACTS 26:9-11 _____

36. What did Paul call Ananias the high priest?

23:3 _____

37. Why did Paul offer an apology?

23:5 _____

38. What special reason may he have had for humbling himself by apologizing?

ROMANS 14:13 _____

Dr. Meyer says: "The best of men are but men at best." Don't try to find perfection in Peter or Paul, or you will be disappointed. We see how far even the excellency of Paul comes short of the behavior of Jesus, who when He was reviled, reviled not again.

39. Is it unscriptural to be righteously indignant?

EPHESIANS 4:26 _____

40. Where should he have stopped short?

ROMANS 12:19 _____

41. What may have been the reason Paul spoke out?

ACTS 23:5 _____

Some lay this to his defective eyesight. Others suggest that Paul's long absence from Jerusalem, or perhaps the seat Ananias occupied, or possibly his failure to have on his distinctive robes, may account for this.

42. What are a Christian's duties to those in authority?

ROMANS 13:1-7 _____

43. What issue did Paul use to throw confusion into the council?

ACTS 23:6 _____

The only sense in which Paul was a Pharisee (now that he was a Christian) was that he believed in a resurrection, yet he knew the Pharisees denied the resurrection he preached. We cannot escape the feeling that this was a device not of the Spirit.

44. What caused a split in the assembly?

23:8, 9 _____

45. What happened to Paul as the result of his scheme?

23:10 _____

_____

46. What message did the Lord send to His servant?

23:11 _____

47. What were Paul's feelings about getting to Rome?

ROMANS 1:9-12 _____

_____

God overruled all these events to give Paul the opportunity to witness, and even when he landed in prison, led him to write some of his most precious epistles.

48. What shows the bitterness of feeling toward Paul?

ACTS 23:12 _____

49. How many Jews entered into this plot?

23:13 _____

50. How did God overrule their diabolical plan?

23:16 _____

This quick-witted, levelheaded, heroic youth took a minor part in God's program, yet how important it was! God can use a humble Christian to upset great calculations of the devil.

51. What did the captain do about this matter?

23:19-22 _____

52. How did God use a boy to equal forty men of Satan?

I CORINTHIANS 1:27 _____

The plan was *too good*. The plotters were so pleased with its clever-
ness that they forgot and talked too loudly. Thus the Lord often causes
clever people to outwit themselves. This youth unconsciously secured
for the church a rich legacy of religious literature. Let us put every
obstacle we can in the way of evil men. We cannot tell how far-reach-
ing may be the results.

53. What precautions were taken to protect Paul?

ACTS 23:23 _____

54. To whom was the case referred?

23:24 _____

55. Why did not the captain handle this case himself?

23:29 _____

56. Where was Paul detained while awaiting his accusers?

23:35 _____

check-up time No. 10

You have just studied some important truths about Acts 21–23. Review your study by rereading the questions and your written answers. If you aren't sure of an answer, reread the Scripture portion given to see if you can find the answer. Then take the following test to see how well you understand important truths you have studied.

In the right-hand margin write "True" or "False" after each of the following statements.

1. The disciples at Tyre told Paul not to go to Jerusalem. _____

2. The Holy Spirit warned Paul of coming affliction. _____

3. Paul took a vow to appease the Jews. _____

4. Paul was a Greek born in Rome. _____

5. Ananias ministered to the needs of the apostle Paul. _____

6. Paul claimed he was a citizen of Jerusalem. _____

7. Paul denounced the high priest in Jerusalem. _____

8. The Pharisees and Sadducees agreed in doctrine. _____

9. The Sadducees believed in the resurrection. _____

10. Paul was sent to Caesarea because of a conspiracy in Jerusalem. _____

Turn to page 96 and check your answers.

Paul in Caesarea

ACTS 24–26

The Witness to Felix—Acts 24

"Conscience void of offence"

1. What professional orator was employed to prosecute?

24:1 _____

2. What impression were his opening remarks supposed to make?

24:2, 3 _____

Two striking things are here revealed. A bad man was credited with good he never did, and a good man with evil deeds he never did.

3. What does the Lord say about flattering lips?

PSALM 12:3 _____

4. What three charges were lodged against Paul?

ACTS 24:5, 6 _____

_____

_____

5. What kind of answer did Paul give?

24:10 _____

79

6. What should all Christians be ready to do?

I Peter 3:15 _____

7. Was Paul guilty of the things of which he was accused?

Acts 24:12 _____

8. What was the one thing lacking in the case?

24:13 _____

9. How did Paul once refer to Christianity?

24:14 _____

10. What had Jesus called it?

John 14:6 _____

Note: Early Christians were often called "the people of the Way."

11. What did Paul have in common with his accusers?

Acts 24:15 _____

12. What had Daniel said about resurrections?

Daniel 12:2 _____

_____

13. What was the teaching of Jesus on this matter?

John 5:28, 29 _____

_____

14. What could Paul say as to his own conscience?

Acts 24:16; cf. 23:1 _____

15. What one thing did Paul have to confess?

24:21 _____

80

16. What did Felix do with the case?

24:22, 23 _____

_____

17. What personal application of the gospel did Paul make?

24:25 _____

18. What excuse did Felix offer?

24:25 _____

19. How long did Felix let the case drag?

24:27 _____

20. What was Paul doing all this time?

24:27 _____

Some say he wrote Ephesians, Philippians, Colossians, and Philemon.

The Witness to Festus—Acts 25

"I appeal unto Caesar"

21. Who were still trying to get Paul out of the way?

25:2 _____

22. What did these leaders want to have done?

25:3 _____

23. What showed that Festus was fair-minded?

25:4 _____

24. What did he require?

25:5 _____

25. What was lacking with all the talk of the accusers?

25:7 _____

26. What did Paul say in his own behalf?

25:8 _____

27. What appeal of Paul's saved him from going to Jerusalem?

25:11 _____

28. Why couldn't the Jews get their way?

Isaiah 14:27 _____

29. Who came to visit Festus?

Acts 25:13 _____

30. What kind of audiences had Jesus promised His apostles?

Mark 13:9 _____

31. What rule for all private censures did Festus state?

Acts 25:16 _____

32. What was Festus' opinion of the Jewish form of worship?

25:19 _____

33. What promise was now being fulfilled?

9:15 _____

34. What was the governor's judgment concerning the case?

25:25 _____

35. Who had given a similar decision?

23:26-30 _____

36. What excuse did Festus make for having King Agrippa hear the case?

25:26 _____

The Witness to Agrippa—Acts 26
"I was not disobedient"

37. For whom did Paul speak when given a chance?

26:1, 15 _____

38. How did Paul feel about this opportunity?

26:2 _____

39. For what did the Jews desire to kill Paul?

26:6, 7 _____

40. What was the seemingly incredible thing about Paul's message?

26:8 _____

41. What answer would Paul give to critics who say that he had a sunstroke?

26:13 _____

42. What occurred in addition to the vision?

26:14 _____

43. Against whom is the sin of persecution registered?

26:15 _____

44. What is the double purpose of preaching?

26:18 _____

45. Why do men remain unsaved?

II CORINTHIANS 4:4 _____

46. If one's sins are forgiven, what does he have?

26:18 _____

47. What happens every time a soul is saved?

26:18; cf. II TIMOTHY 2:26 _____

_____

48. What was Paul's response to the heavenly vision?

ACTS 26:19 _____

49. What good example did Paul set for other Christians?

GALATIANS 1:16 _____

50. What is the mark of true repentance?

ACTS 26:20 _____

51. Of what was Paul not ashamed?

26:22; cf. ROMANS 1:16 _____

Out of five discourses by Paul, two have his personal testimony as a basis. Outside the resurrection of Jesus, the New Testament has no better evidence than the conversion of Saul. Paul well knew that the story of his conversion was worth something to the world.

52. What conclusion had Festus reached?

ACTS 26:24 _____

53. When sinners cannot prove Christianity a bad thing, what do they often try to prove?

II CORINTHIANS 5:13; JOHN 10:20; MARK 3:21 _____

_____

54. Can any sane man turn his back on God's salvation?

LUKE 12:20 _____

55. Of what was Paul assured?

ACTS 26:25 _____

56. Why did Paul not fear to appeal to the facts?

26:26 _____

57. What was the sad response of Agrippa?

26:28 _____

The A.S.V. gives this: "With but little persuasion thou wouldst fain make me a Christian." With this little talk you think you can convince me. This would seem to indicate that Agrippa was not practically persuaded as many have understood it, but that he was mocking Paul for taking it for granted that he was in agreement at all.

58. What was the best thing Paul could wish him?

26:29 _____

The A.S.V. gives this translation: "Whether with little or with much." Whether it needs little or much persuasion, I would have you rejoice in the Christian life as I know it.

59. What was the rulers' only comment among themselves?

26:31 _____

60. What rash thing did they think Paul had done?

26:32 _____

check-up time No. 11

You have just studied some important truths about Acts 24–26. Review your study by rereading the questions and your written answers. If you wish, you may use the self-check test as an aid in reviewing your lesson. If you aren't sure of an answer, reread the Scripture portion given to see if you can find the answer. Then take this test to see how well you understand important truths you have studied.

In the right-hand margin write "True" or "False" after each of the following statements.

1. Tertullus made the accusations against Paul.   _____

2. The Jews proved all the accusations against Paul. _____

3. Felix hoped for a bribe from Paul.   _____

4. Paul appeared also before Festus.   _____

5. Paul wanted to take his case to Caesar.   _____

6. Festus found Paul guilty as charged.   _____

7. King Agrippa allowed Paul to speak for himself.   _____

8. Paul admitted that at one time he persecuted the church.   _____

9. Paul saw a vision at noonday.   _____

10. King Agrippa declared Paul to be innocent.   _____

Turn to page 96 and check your answers.

Paul in Rome

ACTS 27, 28

A Voyager in Peril—Acts 27
"Tossed with a tempest"

Paul had been declared innocent of crime under Roman law by Festus and under Jewish law by Agrippa, but appeal had been made to Caesar and could not be recalled. He must be sent to Rome as God had purposed and the government would pay his traveling expenses. The voyage recounted in this chapter may be taken as typical in many ways of the voyage of life.

1. How was Paul treated by the centurion?

27:3 _____

2. What advice did Paul give the sailors?

27:10 _____

3. How did the captain regard Paul's advice?

27:11 _____

4. What led them to pull up anchor and sail forth?

27:13 _____

5. What do soft south winds usually signify?

I THESSALONIANS 5:3 _____

6. What followed the soft winds?

ACTS 27:14 _____

7. Who controls the winds?

PSALM 135:7; 148:8 _____

8. Who has power to rebuke winds and waves?

MATTHEW 8:23-27 _____

9. What danger is always before those who take their own way instead of God's?

ACTS 27:17 _____

10. What did their human "helps" avail?

27:18 _____

11. What can a child of God always have in outward tempests?

ISAIAH 26:3 _____

12. What is bound to be the result when men drift without a guiding star?

ACTS 27:20 _____

13. What was Paul doing all this time?

27:21 _____

14. To what Bible character was Paul in direct contrast on this occasion?

JONAH 1:5 _____

15. What is ever the attitude of the man who knows God?

PSALM 112:7 _____

16. What assurance was Paul able to give the men?

ACTS 27:22 _____

17. What testimony did Paul give?

27:23, 24 _____

18. What was the secret of Paul's abiding peace?

27:25 _____

19. What influence should a Christian have in such times?

MATTHEW 5:13 _____

20. What did the men do in their impatience?

ACTS 27:29, 30 _____

21. How long had they been without food?

27:33 _____

22. What advice did Paul give?

27:34 _____

23. What assurance did Paul add to that given in 27:24?

27:34 _____

24. What appropriate thing did he do before eating anything?

27:35 _____

25. What was the result of Paul's attitude?

27:36 _____

26. How did they come out of the storm through which they had chosen to sail?

27:40, 41 _____

27. Who defeated the devil's last suggestion for keeping Paul from Rome?

27:43 _____

28. What has God promised to do for all who look to Him in the midst of the shipwrecks of life?

27:44; cf. PSALM 107:28-30 _____

_____

A Preacher in Prison—Acts 28
"By himself with a soldier"

29. Where did they find themselves?

28:1 _____

30. What strange friends did God raise up for them?

28:2 _____

31. How did Paul busy himself when he came ashore?

28:3 _____

32. What was Satan's next device?

28:3 _____

33. What effect did this have on the natives?

28:4 _____

34. How did the Lord give him another opportunity to witness?

28:5 _____

35. To what extreme did popular opinion turn as a result?

28:6 _____

When we see a man of God struggling with a viper, it is a good plan to wait a little before rushing to conclusions. The fact that he is attacked is nothing against him. He may shake it off into the fire.

36. Who became especially interested in Paul?

28:7 _____

37. What blessing resulted from a shipwreck?

28:8, 9 _____

38. How did the inhabitants reward Paul?

28:10 _____

39. How did the Christians in Rome receive Paul?

28:15 _____

40. How was Paul received in official circles?

28:16 _____

41. To whom did Paul appeal in Rome?

28:17 _____

42. From what Scriptures did Paul prove the claims of Christ?

28:23 _____

43. How much of a chance did Paul have to testify?

28:23 _____

44. What prophecy had a fulfillment on this occasion?

ISAIAH 6:9 _____

45. What was Paul's parting word to these Jews?

ACTS 28:25-28 _____

_____

46. What is the spiritual condition of the Jews in general?

28:27 _____

47. What was offered first to Jews and then to the whole world?

28:28 _____

With verse 28 the New Testament curtain falls on the story of Jewish unbelief—probably the reason the history of Acts breaks off at this point. In Rome, the capital of the world, the unbelief of the last section of the Jewish family was manifested, and the gospel branched out to the "uttermost part." The spread of the gospel over the heathen world forms a new chain of history not yet completed.

48. To what subject did Paul stick to the very end?

28:31 _____

According to tradition, Paul was liberated after a successful trial, and went on other journeys, finally being put to death by Nero in the persecution that arose in A.D. 64. It was about that time he wrote his last letter to Timothy, which reads almost like a will.

check-up time No. 12

You have just studied some important truths about Acts 27, 28. Review your study by rereading the questions and your written answers. If you aren't sure of an answer, reread the Scripture portion given to see if you can find the answer. Then take this test to see how well you understand important truths you have studied.

In the right-hand margin write "True" or "False" after each of the following statements.

1. Paul advised the captain to wait for better weather. _____

2. The captain took Paul's advice. _____

3. The ship stopped for lack of wind. _____

4. Paul told them that there would be no loss of life. _____

5. Paul's prediction of shipwreck did not come true. _____

6. A viper fastened itself on Paul's hand. _____

7. Paul healed the father of Publius. _____

8. The shipwrecked crew stayed on the island three months. _____

9. Paul finally arrived in Rome. _____

10. In Rome Paul was immediately put to death. _____

Turn to page 96 and check your answers.

Suggestions for class use

1. The class teacher may wish to tear this page from each workbook as the answer key is on the reverse side.

2. The teacher should study the lesson first, filling in the blanks in the workbook. He should be prepared to give help to the class on some of the harder places in the lesson. He should also take the self-check tests himself, check his answers with the answer key and look up any question answered incorrectly.

3. Class sessions can be supplemented by the teacher's giving a talk or leading a discussion on the subject to be studied. The class could then fill in the workbook together as a group, in teams, or individually. If so desired by the teacher, however, this could be done at home. The self-check tests can be done as homework by the class.

4. The self-check tests can be corrected at the beginning of each class session. A brief discussion of the answers can serve as review for the previous lesson.

5. The teacher should motivate and encourage his students. Some public recognition might well be given to class members who successfully complete this course.

Moody Press, a ministry of the Moody Bible Institute, is designed for education, evangelization and edification. If we may assist you in knowing more about Christ and the Christian life, please write us without obligation to: Moody Press, c/o MLM, Chicago, Illinois 60610.

answer key

to self-check tests

Be sure to look up any questions you answered incorrectly.

Q gives the number of the test *question*.

A gives the correct *answer*.

R *refers* you back to the Scripture reference where the correct answer is to be found.

Mark with an "x" your wrong answers.

	TEST 1		TEST 2		TEST 3		TEST 4		TEST 5		TEST 6	
Q	A	R	A	R	A	R	A	R	A	R	A	R
1	F	1:1	F	3:6	T	6:1	T	7:5	F	9:3	T	13:2
2	F	1:4	T	3:9	T	6:3	F	7:27	T	9:20	F	13:12
3	T	1:5	T	3:21	T	6:4	T	7:35	T	9:40	T	13:23
4	T	1:8	F	4:2	T	6:7	F	7:42	T	10:2	T	13:42
5	T	1:26	T	4:12	T	6:7	T	7:56	F	10:26	T	13:44
6	F	2:1	F	4:20	T	6:10	T	8:5, 6	T	11:15	F	13:52
7	T	2:11	T	4:32	F	6:13	T	8:11	T	11:19	T	14:9,10
8	F	2:16	F	5:2	T	6:13	T	8:18	F	12:5	F	14:19
9	T	2:31	F	5:19	F	6:9, 12	F	8:28	T	12:7	T	14:23
10	F	2:41	T	5:38	T	6:15	T	8:38	F	12:14	F	14:27

	TEST 7		TEST 8		TEST 9		TEST 10		TEST 11		TEST 12	
Q	A	R	A	R	A	R	A	R	A	R	A	R
1	F	15:1	T	16:3	T	19:8	T	21:4	T	24:2	T	27:10
2	F	15:2	F	16:6	T	19:10	T	21:11	F	24:13	F	27:11
3	T	15:4	T	16:14	F	19:16	T	21:26	T	24:26	F	27:18
4	F	15:13	T	16:34	F	19:24	F	22:3	T	25:4	T	27:22
5	T	15:28, 29	F	17:11	T	19:35	T	22:12	T	25:11	F	27:41
6	T	15:28	T	17:22	T	20:9	F	22:25	F	25:25	T	28:3
7	F	15:31	F	17:32	F	20:10	T	23:3	T	26:1	T	28:8
8	F	15:38	F	18:3	T	20:17	F	23:7	T	26:10	T	28:11
9	T	15:39	F	18:11	T	20:22	F	23:8	T	26:13	T	28:16
10	F	15:39	T	18:24	F	20:38	T	23:23	T	26:31	F	28:30

how well
did
you do?

0-1 wrong answers—excellent work

2-3 wrong answers—review errors carefully

4 or more wrong answers—restudy the lesson before going on to the next one